BRAIN WA

CREATIVE WRITING FOR UPPER JUNIORS

Patricia and Steve Harrison

CONTENTS

Notes

This book is designed to build on and extend the materials provided in 'Creative Writing For Lower Juniors.' The categories used are the same so that teachers and pupi ls can recognise continuity of theme. The tasks, levels of writing and text are more challenging reflecting the need for progression. Teacher expectation ought to be higher and it will be useful to examine the quality of work pupils have produced from 'Creative Writing For Lower Juniors' in order to establish higher expectations for the activities in this book.

© 1989 Scholarstown Educational Publishers, on behalf of the authors.

ISBN 1 85276037-0

First published 1989
by Scholarstown Educational Publishers Ltd.
Albert House, Apex Business Centre, Boscombe Road, Dunstable LU5 4RL

Printed in Great Britain at The Bath Press, Avon

Reprinted 1989

Covers by Terry Bambrook
Illustration by Elaine Baker

Acknowledgements
Linda Edmonson and the many teachers and pupils who have trialled these materials with such enthusiasm in such a constructive way.

WHAT IS CREATIVE WRITING?

Creative Writing can be like 'Good Health', it is only when it is not there that we become conscious of how important it is to us. So it was when Curriculum Matters1 'English from 5 to 16 'was produced by HMI[1]. That particular view of English provoked an understandable response from many who regarded it as too inflexible and overly focussed on the functional aspects of language.

The subsequent publication of 'English from 5 to 16, responses to Curriculum Matters 1'[2] recognised those misgivings and cast objectives in much broader terms. This book is concerned with the personal and imaginative writing of children and is consistent with the revised HMI objective of writing
> "descriptions and accounts of personal and of vicarious experience
> which embody both reflection and the expression of feelings"

The Kingman Report [3] reinforces the importance of pupils experimenting with language in response to a variety of stimuli. The personal nature of the response is the central notion.

" In practice, in the classroom, 'English for personal development' means, for example, children writing their own verse and fiction .... quite apart from all the humanistic reasons for encouraging pupils to write stories and poems, there are sound linguistic reasons, because the activity gives them the opportunity to experiment with language, trying out forms they would otherwise never use. Some of the structures of written language allow us to assemble our thoughts and to link our ideas in ways that are not so readily available in everyday spontaneous speech."

As teachers we ought not to make apologies for using terms such as 'creative writing'. The capacity to respond in an imaginative, personal and unique way to a variety of stimuli is surely a human characteristic we ought to celebrate. There is no reason why the televised image should dominate pupils' lives and if we wish to encourage imagination we need opportunities and vehicles for its expression.

Children as writers need opportunities to practise their craft. They will benefit from such opportunities in what they learn about themselves and the unique contribution they can offer. They will realise their potential for creating experiences which others can share and in so doing they can grow both in confidence and fluency.

The materials provided in this book are not intended to substitute for the expression of feeling and imagination across the curriculum. Empathy and insights can develop through History, Geography, R.E. and other curriculum areas. Similarly, unplanned occurrences ought to be capitalised upon by all teachers who recognise the essential place of spontaneity in teaching. However beware of the rabbit at the window syndrome!

Children vary in their abilities to write and to use their imagination. We have attempted in this book of photocopy free sheets to try and stimulate pupils' imaginations and to harness the resulting responses in a variety of ways.

1. English from 5 to 16. Curriculum matters 1. An HMI Series.. HMSO 1984
2. English from 5 to 16. Response to Curriculum Matters 1. An HMI Report. HMSO 1986
3. Report Of the Committee Of Inquiry Into The Teaching Of English Language. HMSO 1988 P 10.

WHAT IS CREATIVE WRITING?

Classroom Approaches

No doubt many of us at sometime or other have carved out a breathing space by setting a creative writing task at a moment's notice. As a survival technique it is understandable but it is impossible to justify educationally.

'Creative Writing' has suffered badly from allegations of lack of clear objectives, woolly classroom organisation and a lack of structure. In using the contents of this book we therefore suggest the teacher considers a number of possible classroom techniques and organisational approaches.

Children are authors when engaged in creative writing. The creativity provides a unique character to the work not present in other aspects of English language work. It is important therefore to model the pupil activity on that of authors in general. In writing any piece we begin with an outline draft of the final object. Ideas can be agreed and key vocabulary identified. The time devoted to such pre-planning will vary according to the age and ability of the writer but it ought to be there. It need not all be written, a dialogue with the teacher and/or other pupils will be of great benefit in many cases, allowing the child to verbalise ideas and in so doing to refine and clarify a plan of action. It is worth considering providing pupils with a notebook which is specifically for such planning purposes. The same book may contain the key words the child intends to introduce into the story, in many cases these may have been cross-checked either with an adult or by using a dictionary.

Beware however that the trappings of authorship do not smother the central idea of what the child wants to say, too much pre-planning with pupils who are not ready can turn off even the most enthusiastic. On occasions it is valid for a group of children to be given the same task. The identification of key words can then become a group activity. A suitable display (e.g. a word tree) can be developed from which pupils will choose words appropriate to their own particular responses.

A Word Tree

Writers in schools

One of the most effective ways of stimulating pupils to write is to expose them to 'real writers'. Often authors in school will bring examples of their draft copies, the 'secrets ' of colour separation for printing, the need to check text before final print etc. They also provide adult models in the way they enthuse about their craft and the enjoyment writing brings to them personally. Many schools can obtain financial assistance for writers in school and if not already doing so should seriously consider providing such an experience for pupils.

To Choose or Not to Choose

In developing a range of pupil skills in writing we cannot abdicate our responsibility to provide opportunities using a variety of stimuli. Nor however should we be so directive as to deprive the pupil of any element of choice. Some stimuli may not prove effective with certain pupils. This may apply only at a certain time and offered on other occasions may fire imaginations. In attempting to provide a balance we suggest pupils have some degree of choice from the range available.

WHAT IS CREATIVE WRITING?

Audience

The question of 'why' we are writing is central. Sometimes we may compose poetry, keep a diary or write a short story solely for personal pleasure. On other occasions we write in the hope that others can share our thoughts and feelings. In school the audience may be a small group, a class, the whole school, parents or even the world.

In sharing our writing with others we may develop personal anthologies, class story books, school publications or contribute to a collection across a district. Increasingly we might seek to translate the written word so as to communicate it in some other way through mime, drama, music or art. One form of creative expression giving birth to another.

Teachers not already doing so should consider the potential of the word processor for the planning, drafting, re-drafting and eventual final product of the child's writing.

Feedback

James Joyce would never have had 'Ulysses' published if punctuation was always of greater significance than style, imagination and creativity. Then again Joyce was capable of writing a novel with standard punctuation and chose not to do so. If one intention of creative writing is to provide enjoyment for an audience then clearly that audience needs to be able to comprehend the message the author is offering. As ever a middle road is possible. In providing feedback to the pupil we should consider offering comments in two main categories. The first is the quality of the idea and its creative expression. The second is the way in which it is communicated. It is important not to drown creativity in a sea of grammar, punctuation and spelling correction but it is also important to recognise that communicating ideas requires a common set of shared structures. It is highly desirable to engage pupils in a degree of self-appraisal. Equally the reaction of a peer group is to be valued in providing feedback for the writer.

Teacher support is a matter for professional judgements in context, however a number of considerations ought to be borne in mind. The tone of the classroom is crucial. The teacher must transmit to the child that what s/he has to say is worth saying and will be valued by the teacher. Explicitly or implicitly the message "I want to know what you think and I value your opinions" must be received by the pupil.

The same is true of teacher intervention. Unless children are encouraged to elaborate, be more precise and develop a range of expression there is the danger that some will churn out the same core vocabulary in the same style 'ad infinitum'.

The Photocopy Masters

The focus throughout is on imagination and story. Other forms of descriptive writing can be found in the companion books 'Writing for Specific Purposes'. In developing the materials used in this book we have attempted to provide variety both in format and in the thrust of the stimulus. Each section has a different focus but that is not to imply that the learning process is rigidly compartmentalised. The main focus of one section will be present to a lesser degree in other sections.

We would suggest a balance of sheets is offered over a period of time. It would be unwise to work through one category and then another, far better to mix the styles of pupil work. This also allows the teacher to reflect on progress and development in pupil use of vocabulary, structures and ideas. This is often easier to discern if the first few sheets are filed and later compared with sheets used some time afterwards. Such comparisons can be useful for demonstrating development to the children and encouraging them to build on past successes.

WRITING FROM THE CHARACTER'S POINT OF VIEW.

Focus of development

This book attempts to provide a range of experiences and emotions to the writing 'from a character's point of view'. Each photocopy master emphasises a different aspect of human action or feelings - ranging from injustice to concern for others. It will be beneficial if teachers discuss these with pupils and allow them to reflect on moments in their own lives when such emotions have been experienced.

Individual Masters

6 The central theme is injustice. Many pupils, rightly or wrongly, will have experienced a sense of injustice in their day to day lives. This will generate lively discussion. Invite them to think of other examples they know of injustice. The question moves on to 'choices' and here again the pros and cons, rights and wrongs of various choices can be explored.

7 Despite their relatively young age, children can nevertheless regard themselves as 'old' relative to younger siblings and friends. They are certainly capable of reflecting on their own lives. Trials with this material produced an enormous range of unexpected feelings of guilt and regret. One girl regretted how much she enjoyed playing football because she believed it was 'not normal'. The opportunity for discussion and sympathetic support from teachers is wide ranging.

8 Curiosity is a major element in a child's formative years. This photocopy master will benefit from preliminary discussion of the temptations curiosity brings and the choices faced when deciding whether or not to 'give in' or to 'resist' temptation.

9 Most children harbour ambitions about the future. These often seem unrealistic but there are many examples of the rich and famous who were told that their ambitions had no hope of being realised! An aspect of this sheet is the preparation, single-mindedness and dedication needed if ambitions are to be realised . The writing need not be overly concentrated on the 'likely', we all need to dream of the future at sometime. Many children may not relish the prospect of being a famous dancer. The work can be developed into what they would like to be.

10   Concern for others runs through much of our work in school. This sheet encourages pupils to produce imaginative work with the thread of caring underpinning it.

11 We all have forebodings, sometimes in our dreams, sometimes simply feelings. It often helps to write about them in order to exorcise them. Children can extend this work by discussing and writing about their own particular forebodings.

12 This sheet provides an initial sense of frustration. How do you convince someone that you are who you claim to be? - This is an opportunity to develop the unique character of the individual - 'What is it that makes me who I am, etc?

13 The totally unexpected and its 'shock' effect is a stock-in-trade of books and movies. Children have little difficulty imagining the situation. The teacher needs to encourage originality and a careful use of vocabulary. The danger is that the responses will be too alike unless pupils are advised to think and write with real flair.

14   Initial discussion should centre on who they would most/least like to see through the magnifying glass.

15 Characters from mythology can be researched as part of the identification with a specific personality. Those on this sheet are drawn from the Greek tradition, some pupils may be interested in discovering their Roman equivalents. There are also interesting parallels with Hindu mythology and such a development will allow a consideration of why these characters reflect a range of qualities and emotions.

WANTED

DEAD OR ALIVE

The wildest kid in the West

Name _____

REWARD $5,000

• Draw your self-portrait on the poster

• Write your name on the line.

• You have done nothing wrong.

• Describe your actions.
Do you give yourself up?
Try to escape?
Fight it out?

_____

_____

_____

_____

_____

_____

_____

If you could start your life again, what would you change about it, and why?

_____

_____

_____

_____

_____

_____

_____

_____

_____

BEHIND THE LOCKED DOOR

Why did Uncle Jim always keep that room locked?

One day he was called out to an emergency.

He forgot to take the key.

Describe what happened to you from entering the room until Uncle Jim's return.

_____

_____

_____

continue overleaf ▶

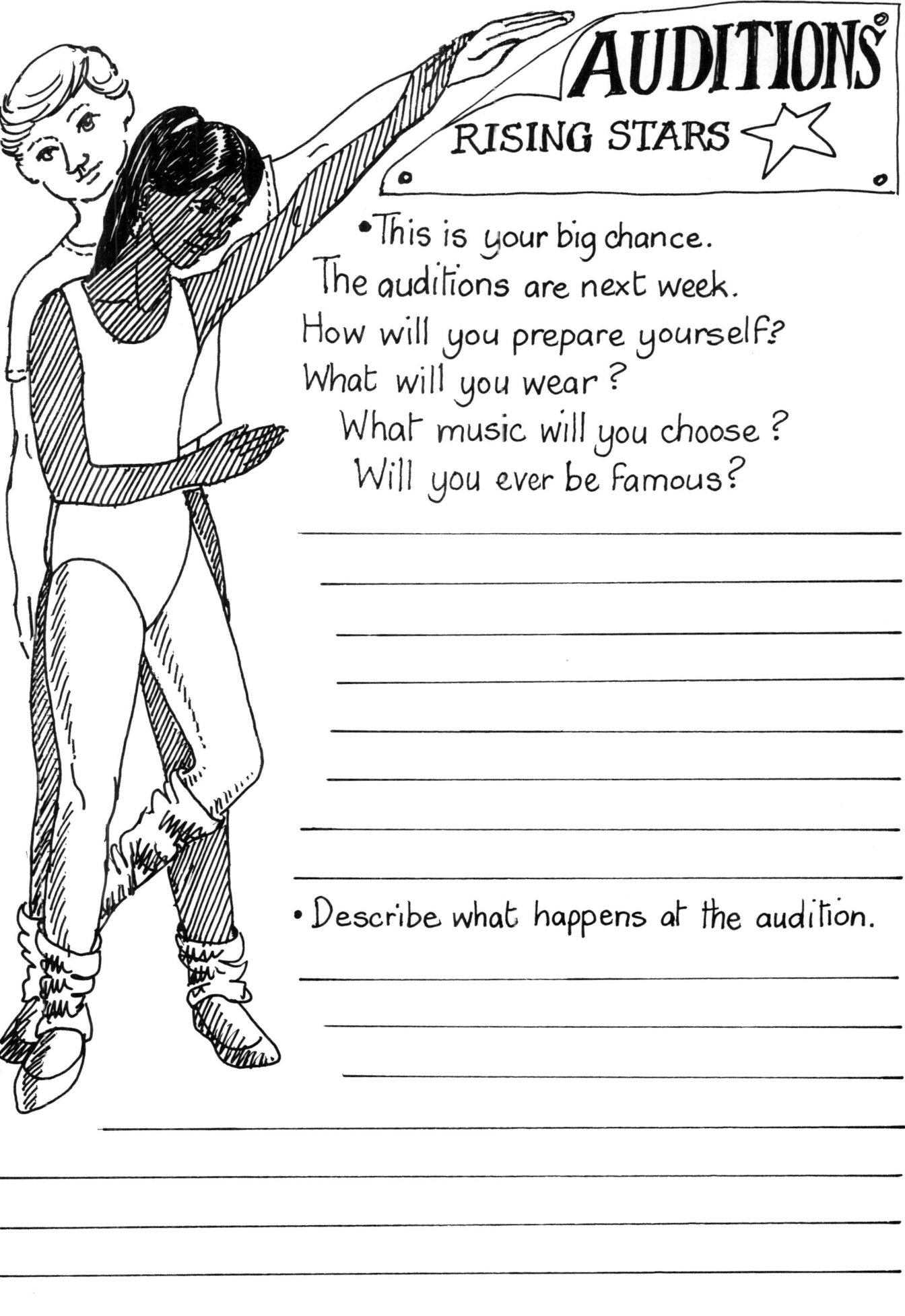

AUDITIONS
RISING STARS

• This is your big chance.
The auditions are next week.
How will you prepare yourself?
What will you wear?
What music will you choose?
Will you ever be famous?

_____

_____

_____

_____

_____

_____

• Describe what happens at the audition.

_____

_____

_____

_____

_____

_____

_____

SLEEPWALK

It is 3 a.m. The haunting music drifts through the night air. Your brother seems to be in a trance. You follow.
• What happens?
• What do you do?

_____

_____

_____

_____

_____

_____

_____

_____

Imagine that you are the child in the locked cellar.

• How did you get there?   • Why are you there?
• How will you get out?   IF AT ALL!

_____

_____

_____

_____

_____

_____

_____

_____

_____

DOUBLE TROUBLE

Another child has moved into your home, looking exactly like you. Your parents think **YOU** are the alien clone.

• What can you do?

How can you convince them that you are their real child?

_____

_____

_____

_____

_____

_____

_____

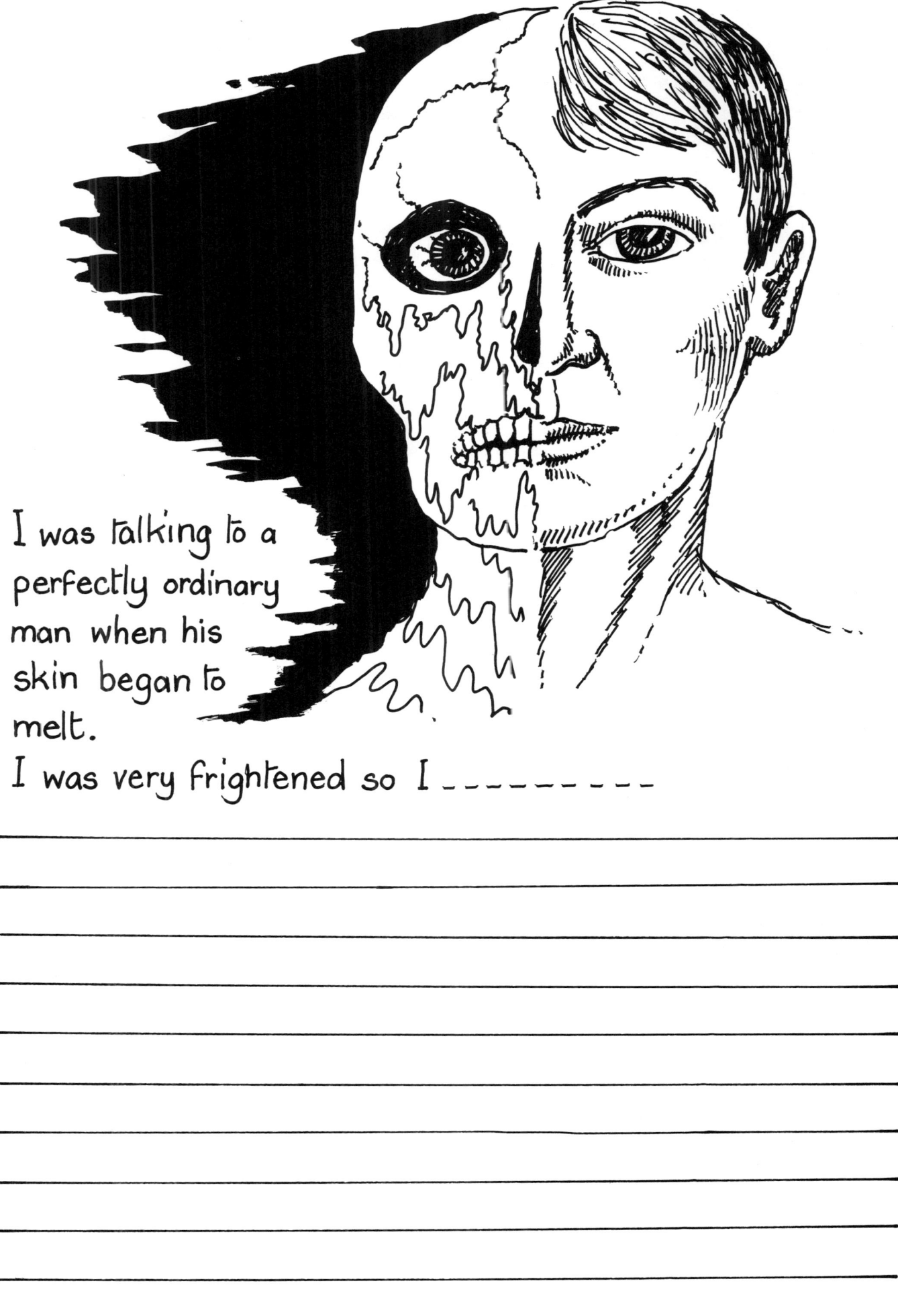

I was talking to a
perfectly ordinary
man when his
skin began to
melt.

I was very frightened so I _ _ _ _ _ _ _ _ _ _

_____

_____

_____

_____

_____

_____

_____

_____

_____

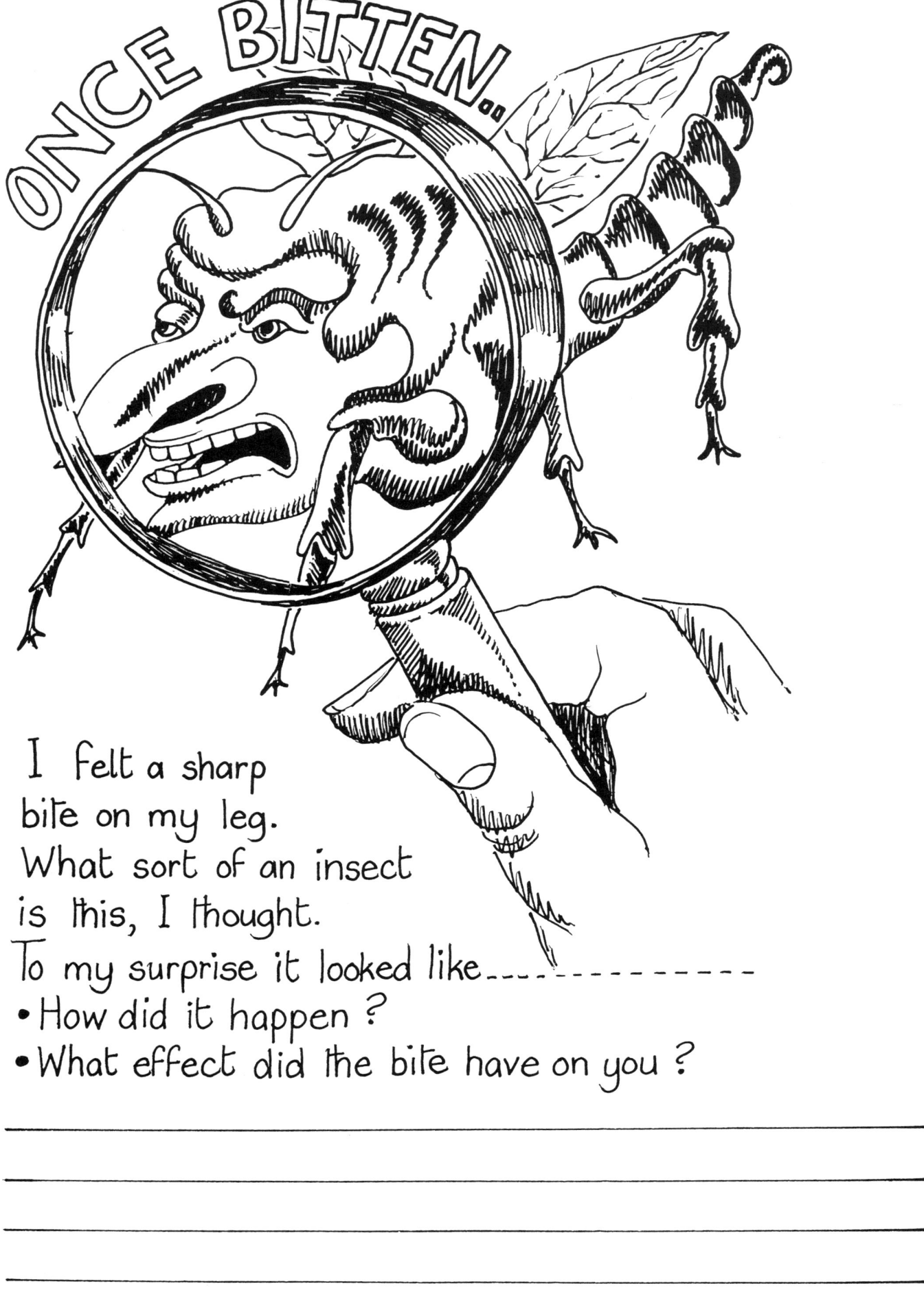

ONCE BITTEN..

I felt a sharp
bite on my leg.
What sort of an insect
is this, I thought.
To my surprise it looked like _ _ _ _ _ _ _ _ _ _ _ _ _ _
• How did it happen ?
• What effect did the bite have on you ?

_____

_____

_____

_____

_____

continue overleaf ▶

If you dare put on a mask you enter another world.
Which mask would you choose ?

• Describe what happens when you do.

_____

_____

_____

_____

_____

_____

_____

_____

_____

'SPEECH BUBBLES'

Focus of Development

'Creative Writing For Lower Juniors' drew attention to the value of speech bubbles for producing a narrative effect which is not focussed on the 'I'.

The sheets in this book develop that theme but take it further. The speech bubbles are linked to a story which the child must tell. They also build up to four characters speaking about the same event, this requires much more than the dialogue which 'Creative Writing For Lower Juniors' introduced.

The other development is in the use of thought bubbles as an alternative to speech bubbles. At first sight speech and thought are very similar but on reflection they are fundamentally different and this can be demonstrated through the pupil writing.

Individual Masters

17 Teacher - pupil discussion can concentrate on the contexts in which we speak and the effect of the context on what we say. Related to pupils' own experiences, many examples will be forthcoming. Examples may be of domestic, street, school or games experiences. The important point is that what and how we speak is often context determined and context-specific. Thus this Sheet can initiate a discussion not only on what the tennis player might say at the moment of conflict but what he might say 10 or 30 minutes later.

The second part of the task requires the children to develop a scenario which could result in such an outcome.

18/19 In these sheets we can develop the differences between what we think and what we actually say. How often have we as adults fumed internally and yet remained restrained and polite in our actual speech?

Children should discuss this at length. It is a vital social skill both for determining our behaviour but also for understanding the hidden message of what others may say.

These sheets should concentrate initially on the thoughts. The results of this in trials was a very wide range of responses which benefited from subsequent discussion and pupils sharing their ideas.

The second task, to describe what has happened, allows for a wide variety of responses from the 'she forgot' variety to the 'saving of a child in the canal' type response. Finally the pupils must predict what will follow.

20 Class/group discussion needs to develop the importance of caring for others and the scandal of unwanted and neglected pets.

The writing will help to develop a child's ability to convince through the written word, which requires careful planning and the construction of an argument.

21 Most children should know this story but if there are some who don't they will need access to it. The story has a 'twist' added to it. The irony of the ugly sister's foot fitting the shoe.

The speech bubbles allow for four different points of view to be expressed and require the children to put themselves into the shoes of the four different characters! They ought not to identify with any one but should attempt to reflect the feelings of each.

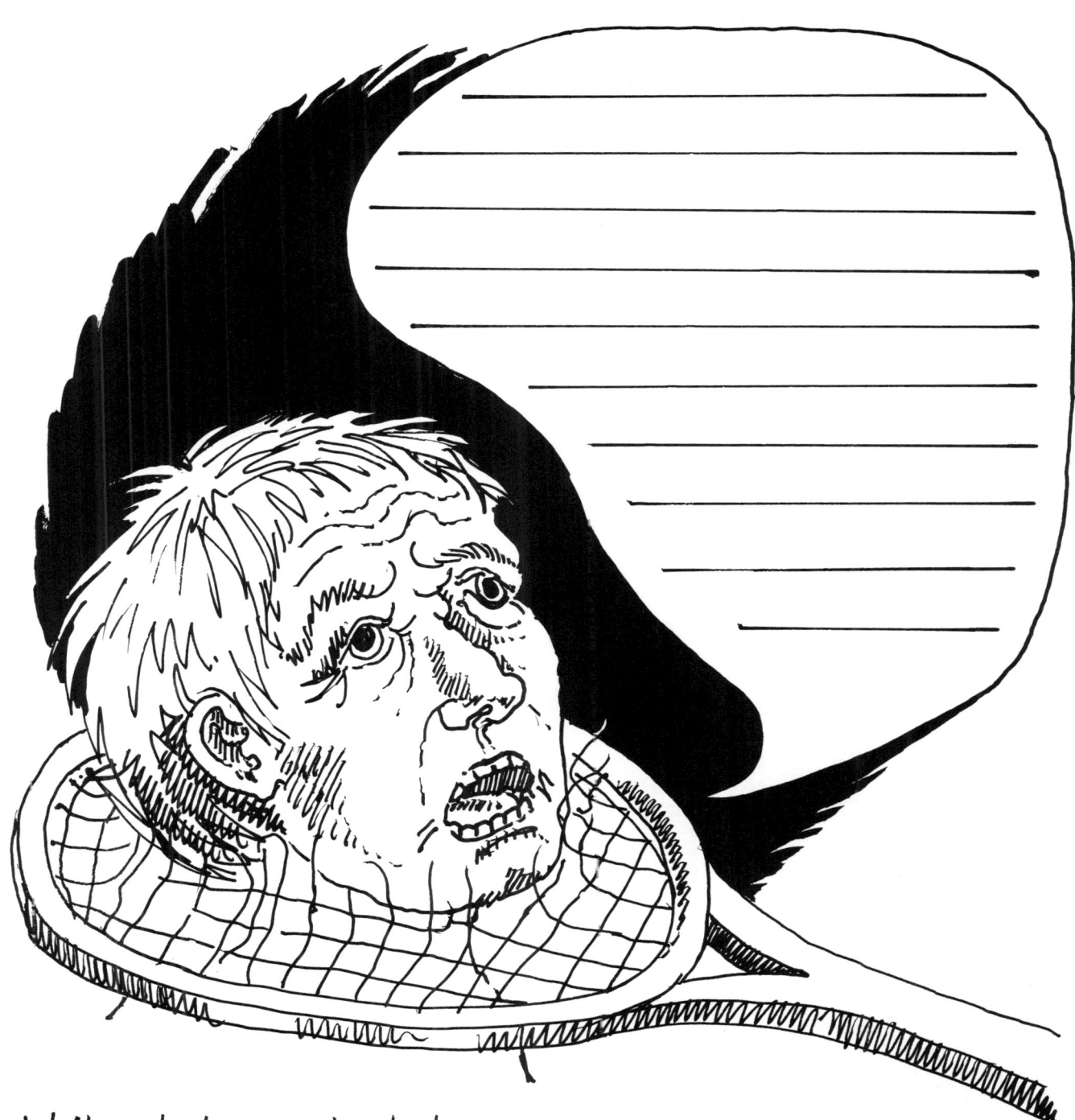

• Write what you think he is saying.
• Describe a game of tennis you have just watched which ended like this.

_____

_____

_____

_____

_____

continue overleaf ▶

May be photocopied for classroom use only.   CWU. Sheet 17

The wedding is fixed for 2pm.
- Write what each of them is thinking.
- Describe what you think has happened.
- What will happen next?

Surprise Surprise

The prince was amazed.

One of the ugly sisters had the same size feet as Cinderella, and she tried the slipper on first.

• What is each person saying?

• Complete the story in an amusing way.

May be photocopied for classroom use only.

DESCRIPTIVE WRITING FROM IMAGINATION.

Focus of Development

The essential points are that the writer is here an observer who does not participate or, with teacher encouragement, is a participant who is not the central character but who observes events from a short distance. Discussion and follow up should highlight the different approaches, structures and vocabulary we use in adopting a different style.

This book, however, concentrates on two clear approaches. One is where the illustration serves as the key to the story. Picture interpretation is paramount and the starting point is at the pupil's discretion. The other approach is where the opening lines are provided and the pupil picks up the story and continues it.

Individual Masters

23 Many novels, short stories and movies feature the bookcase device. 'The Lion the Witch and the Wardrobe' starts from a piece of bedroom furniture and leads into a superb tale. The bookcase is therefore simply an opening onto whatever fantasy the child wishes to develop. This particular sheet has been used by some children as a starting point for their own mini.novel, with a series of chapters, adventures, characters and developments. Some schools have used it as a catalyst for a group to write a book, each child contributing a chapter or section.

24 There are two aspects of this sheet which will benefit from teacher attention. In terms of the writing it is important to discuss with the pupils the imposition of 'time' on the events. Many children write as if time has no significance. It is valuable, on occasions to put a 'timing' on to the period over which events occur. The 40 minutes in this case can be supported by a style of writing which logs the times - this is a supportive mechanism for pupils who need it. e.g. I8.15 Millie heard ....
I8.20 She realised .... etc.
The other element which may benefit from discussion is the gender of the child called upon to save the 'plane'. The basic question of whether assumptions are made about whether a boy would be expected to take control can be aired and pupil attitudes explored.

25 The opening lines are provided. Children can be encouraged to draw other characters from the rather bizarre orchestra.

26 There is a need here for consideration of motive. Much pupil writing concentrates on describing **what** happened. Here there is an important consideration of the **why** of the action. What might have happened to make the driver behave in this way? Could it be related to the pupils he carries each day or is it a separate cause?

27 A straightforward fantasy but school based. Preliminary discussion could consider where people might hide and why they would choose one location over another. This activity also lends itself to drama work. The location is the school and therefore the classroom is itself the stage.

28 The imaginative work for this sheet requires the children to start from the discovery and to work back from the evidence of the discovery in order to reconstruct the past.
There is a free choice in terms of what is discovered but subsequent writing should be consistent with the object or objects the archaeologist has uncovered.

This is a very appropriate use of imagination. Many historians and archaeologists have (and still do) used their imaginations creatively in reconstructing the past from evidence discovered.

The bookcase swung open. The secret passage was dark. There were cobwebs, stone steps and beyond....
....darkness.

Tell the tale of the journey down the secret passage.

BEYOND THE BOOKCASE

_____

_____

_____

_____

_____

_____

_____

_____

_____

When I was offered the job of pianist at the interview, I could not believe my ears, I was delighted, but I had not met the rest of the orchestra.

Describe what happened at the first performance.

_____

_____

_____

continue overleaf ▶

Every morning he drove the bus to school. It was a boring journey along streets of ordinary houses, ordinary shops and very ordinary people. This morning was totally extraordinary.

- Why did the driver do it?
- Describe what happened on this extraordinary journey.

_____

_____

_____

_____

_____

_____

continue overleaf ▶

"Won't you come out and talk to us?" croaked a voice from the strange shape hovering above the school. We looked at each other and decided it was safer inside.

This did not satisfy the invaders.

• Write about what happened next.

_____

_____

_____

_____

_____

_____

_____

continue overleaf ▶

- What exciting discovery has the archaeologist made?
- What does it tell you about the past?
- Describe the event that happened there long ago.

_____

_____

_____

_____

_____

_____

_____

_____

_____

_____

_____

continue overleaf ▶

SEQUENCING EVENTS

Focus of Development

'Creative Writing For Lower Juniors' indicated the value of sequencing in establishing a pattern to story telling. Stories can be the written equivalent of a series of visual snapshots. In looking for a beginning, middle and end to our stories we can benefit from the example of a picture sequence. The task is developed in this book by removing some of the contextual props and placing the onus on pupils to order their own work.

It is worthwhile cutting up strip cartoons and asking pupils to put them back together in their correct sequence. The discussion that follows can concentrate on the degree to which clues about sequence were primarily visual or textual. Different cartoons from different sources may well lead to varying conclusions. This section lends itself to group discussion and planning and to the use of tape recorders to tell the story as the picture sequence unfolds.

Individual Masters

30 The task requires pupils to construct a story from five pictures. The pictures are open to a wide variety of interpretation and can therefore be arranged in a number of different orders to make coherent stories. The end results should be shared. Some pupils will interpret the three children as hostile and threatening whereas others may see them as friendly and helpful. This provides an opportunity for debate about how and why we make judgments.

The well known story that when a white man runs through the suburbs of New York he is assumed to be a jogger but when a black man runs through he is assumed to be a mugger illustrates for us the importance of examining the context for our judgements.

31 No limit or advice is given to the child in terms of the number of pictures which can be drawn. It is a point which will benefit from teacher-pupil discussion e.g.'what criteria should be used for deciding the number and detail of pictures?'

The description of events ought to follow debate about the relationship of text to picture. 'Is it a waste of time to describe in words what the picture already shows?' 'Should the description of events flesh-out the visual sequence and if so what kind of detail is appropriate?'

32 The picture sequence is very easy to follow. The' what could happen next' may be beyond the experience of many pupils and will be helped by group discussion of possible outcomes. Once completed this story can not only be taped and matched to the pictures but can be written up as dialogue and narrative and developed as drama.

33 Sequence is still the theme and the diary continues an approach introduced in 'Creative Writing For Lower Juniors'. The task however is not easy. The complexity of everything working in reverse is mind-boggling, even the words on the diary might be written sdrawkcab!

The teacher will need to use professional judgment in determining the elements which should feature in the reverse sequence. Many pupils do respond very positively to this challenge.

The task can be extended for those who are imaginative and capable of further development into the reversal of other time scales; a week, a year, or a life. 'Born an eighty year old we progress towards, infancy' is an extension that has delighted many children and resulted in exciting writing.

- Cut out the 5 pictures.
- Arrange them in an order which you can use to tell an exciting story.
- Write the story.

- Draw a picture sequence to show what happens next.
- Describe the events.

- Complete the picture sequence.
- Write a story to match the pictures.

Imagine that time worked the other way. **BACK IN TIME**
At 9 pm in the evening you would eat
breakfast. Cars and buses would drive
in reverse. We would all walk
backwards.
• Draw the events of the day.

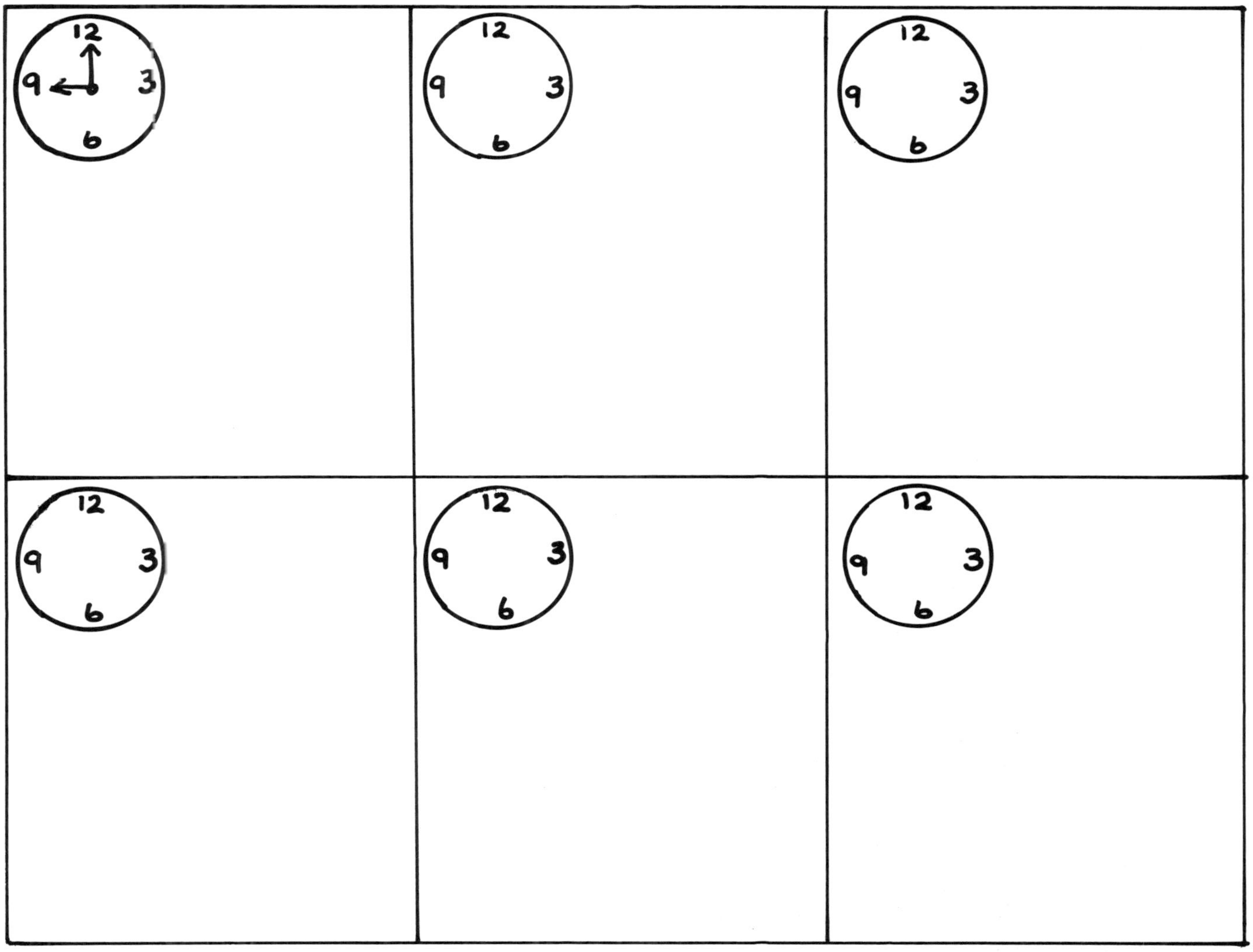

• Write a day's diary. Describe your problems.

p.m.	a.m.
_____	_____
_____	_____
_____	_____
_____	_____

continue overleaf ▶

Focus of Development
The potential of these sheets as stimuli for longer stories in chapter form ought to be explored. Teachers should consider carefully the aspect of 'audience' at this point. It is legitimate to add to the task outlined on the sheet a specific target audience. This requires discussion but will concentrate pupils' minds on the purpose of their story telling and will inform their judgements about vocabulary, style, approach and length. Writing, telling or taping stories for younger children not only extends storywriting skills but also more general communication skills. Many of the sheets can be adapted for group work in drama which will add an oral dimension to what may otherwise be a largely written exercise.

Individual Masters
35 One possible pitfall which will need to be avoided in this exercise is that pupils will all opt to write themselves into the same t.v. programmes and that those programmes may be selected without too much thought for the potential of the child's participation. Preliminary discussion about possible programmes and the child's role in them will be valuable.

36 Pupils may like to have access to the traditional stories about genies in bottles and the exploits they and their owners become involved in. The ownership of this bottle is an open question which pupils can address if they feel the story should develop along those lines.

37 The pupil response to these tasks can be usefully compared to previous results for similar activities. This will assist in judgements about the writer's development and progress.

38 Background research on Neptune will contribute to the quality of the story. Neptune's role, character and disposition will all have implications for Neville and may be used by Neville in his response to the situation. As with the masks of Greek mythology encountered in sheet 10 pupils may wish to learn more of the various gods of the sea from the different classical traditions.

39 The focus of this sheet is in stark contrast to many of the others. It is set in the real world which many pupils will know either personally or vicariously. As such it can usefully be part of a wider discussion on what concerns pupils in their environment. Many young children are afraid on the streets, often with good reason. Some will have personal experiences on which to draw and all such discussion will assist in the establishment of the 'realistic' setting in which the events take place.

40 Teachers may like to undertake this exercise themselves by imagining an exchange with the local director of education or even the Secretary of State.

In the classroom it can result in highly imaginative and hilarious story telling. Years of discontent can surface through the righting of perceived wrongs. Invariably the child as teacher is autocratic, attracted to draconian measures and keen on corporal punishment. Whatever the outcomes there is enormous scope for discussion after the writing in order to explore the implications of the child's model of a classroom where roles are reversed.

41 The teacher will need to consider how far s/he wishes the story to be set in a realistic environment. Where this is considered desirable it will require research into where dangerous sharks live and their habits. This can provide a well researched background for a fantasy. If this approach is followed it is valuable to discuss with pupils the care some authors take to research fully the setting of their story so that while the plot may be fiction its setting is realistic, thereby making the whole more plausible and attractive to readers.

42 Make sure pupils have access to the story, the second part can use any story. The writer must make changes to the events and to the ending.

43 This sheet is rooted in reality. It requires discussion of the pros and cons of taking different types of action. Again it lends itself to dramatic reconstruction.

Aysha's wish was granted. All of a sudden she was on the screen with her favourite characters.

• Imagine it happened to you.
Write a script for a popular TV programme and add yourself to the cast.

_____

_____

_____

_____

continue overleaf ▶

BOTTLED UP!

- Write a story.

Consider------

How did she get there?

How does she feel?

How might she get out? How might she exact her revenge?

_____

_____

_____

_____

continue overleaf ▶

• Complete the story

Neville didn't believe in Neptune, the Roman god of the sea, but his mind was changed when _

_____

_____

_____

_____

continue overleaf ▶

They ran around the corner. It was darker here, not many street lights. They pulled up looking for somewhere to hide.

Finish this story. Why are they hiding? Who from? What will happen if they are found?

_____

_____

_____

_____

_____

_____

_____

_____

All change

• If only it were possible!
Tell the story of a day when adults and children changed places.

_____

_____

_____

_____

_____

continue overleaf ▶

PICNIC

Complete the story---

It was time to leave when we saw them _ _ _ _ _ _ _ _ _ _

_____

_____

_____

_____

_____

_____

_____

_____

_____

_____

- Does Karen enter the book with the Lilliputians?
Would you?
- Choose your favourite story. Write a new ending with
you in it.

_____

_____

_____

_____

_____

_____

_____

_____

Amadip and Jenny have spotted the car reported stolen the day before.

• What will they do? What will be the outcome?

  Write an exciting account of the events.

_____

_____

_____

_____

_____

continue overleaf ▶

FUN WITH WORDS

Focus of Development
The whole thrust of this final section is away from reality and into an exploration and experimentation with words and phrases. Classroom display can be utilised to support the theme and pupils encouraged to discuss with family and friends some sayings and their meanings which are used locally. The enjoyment to be derived from words is a key aspect of this section.

Individual Masters
45 The link word is 'time'. Having matched text to pictures pupils should attempt to write a sentence which makes the meaning clear. Some pupils may find this rather difficult, in which case they should write what they think it means in their own words before attempting to include the phrase in a sentence.

Similar exercises can be developed using a different 'key' word. The teacher could provide a number of sentences but a challenging alternative is to give the pupils a key word and ask them to research as many phrases as possible which include that word (e.g. Jack - 'before you can say Jack Robinson', 'Jack of all trades' etc.)

46 Sheet 36 takes a similar theme but does not require a matching exercise. Nor are pupils expected to write single sentences which illuminate the meaning. Instead they are asked to write continuous prose which includes the phrases. Teachers may prefer some pupils to demonstrate an understanding of the 'mind' phrases before attempting the story.

47 A popular extension to the anagram sheet is to ask children to make up their own sentences and try them out on friends.

48 The Limerick is to be found in many anthologies and in a wide variety of schoolbooks. Pupils should hear some, read some, have them on display around the room and then embark on writing their own. It is useful to link different ones with a common theme (placenames, peoples names, animals etc.) and to produce a selection for display or for printing in the school newspaper.

TIME AFTER TIME

- Write these phrases next to the correct picture.

A stitch in time · Killing time
In between time · Time is up
Time after time · Dead time
Time flies · Half time

- Draw pictures for these phrases.
Out of time · Closing time
Before time · Full time

- Put each phrase in a sentence to make the meaning clear.

"TWO MINDS ARE BETTER THAN ONE"

- Draw amusing pictures for each of these phrases.

A mind of his own.

Mind over matter.

Great minds think alike.

I'm in two minds.

I've half a mind to ____

Out of sight out of mind.

Give you a piece of my mind.

- Write a story which includes as many of these phrases as possible.

_____

_____

_____

_____

_____

_____

_____

_____

continue overleaf ▶

Warren shaved his bread

To make sense the sentence should say—————— "Warren shaved his beard."

<u>Beard</u> is an anagram of <u>bread.</u> The same letters make two different words.

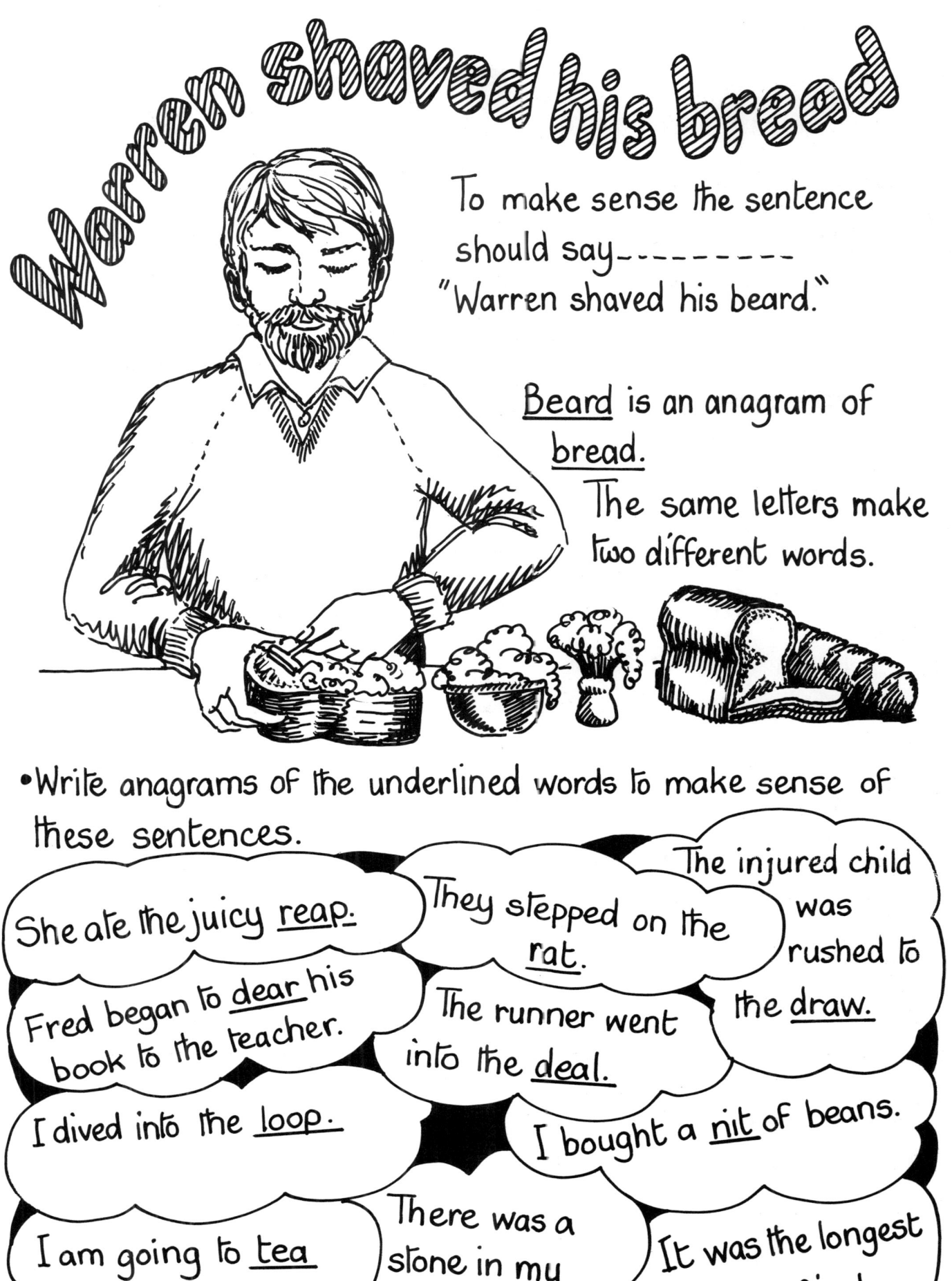

• Write anagrams of the underlined words to make sense of these sentences.

She ate the juicy <u>reap.</u>

They stepped on the <u>rat.</u>

The injured child was rushed to the <u>draw.</u>

Fred began to <u>dear</u> his book to the teacher.

The runner went into the <u>deal.</u>

I dived into the <u>loop.</u>

I bought a <u>nit</u> of beans.

I am going to <u>tea</u> my <u>eat.</u>

There was a stone in my <u>lump.</u>

It was the longest <u>plea</u> in the final.

An active young farmer from Surrey
Left the house in a terrible hurry
He dashed round the bend
And there met his end
When he fell in a pit of fresh slurry.

LIMERICKS

• Draw a three picture sequence for these limericks.

A young trainee gardener from Leeds
Was sorting through three tons of seeds
A gust of wind came
Was followed by rain
Now Leeds can't be seen for the trees.

There was a strange woman from Crewe
Who drank inky tea from a shoe
Though it tasted quite nice
She paid a high price
When, alas, it turned her bright blue.

• Choose a local placename
and write your own limerick.
It helps if you make a list
of rhyming words first
eg. DUNDEE rhymes with

Sea	Me
Pea	See
Free	
Flea	
Tree	